AF454108

Evidence of Hope
A Personal Healing Journey Captured with Art

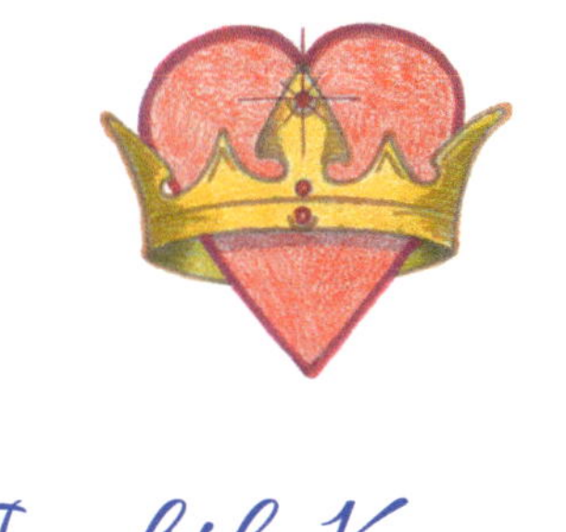

Judith Kayadoe
Royalty Fine Art

Scripture quotations are taken from the ESV® Bible (The Holy Bible, English Standard Version®), copyright © 2001 by Crossway, a publishing ministry of Good News Publishers. Used by permission. All rights reserved.

Translation help: Lin Jane Kosinski Maynard
Print formatting: Jody Skinner, skinnerselfpub.com

Dedication

Dedicated to Jesus and my husband Jimmy, my heroes,
and to all survivors of satanic ritual abuse.
May you have a close relationship with Jesus
and be restored and renewed by Him.

Contents

In this book, I captured little pieces of my healing journey with Jesus. A few years ago, I received one of my first prophecies. (A prophecy is a divinely inspired foretelling of what is to come.) What it said was that I would be an example to show others that there is hope. So that became the title of this book. This prophecy also said that I am a bridge between heaven and earth to convey to earth what happens in heaven. I have held on to this prophecy in the very hard years I have been through because, in the harshest moments and days, it reminded me that everything was going to be all right.

I would like to briefly share some parts of my story.

From a very young age, I was trapped in satanism. At the age of six, I was in a ceremony, surrounded by many people. They were all dressed in black with their heads covered so it wasn't easy to recognize anyone. I was being chosen by satan to be his bride, to be set apart to satan, because he had big plans for me. Toward the end of the ceremony, satan forced me to make a choice. I could be tortured in the most horrible ways, or I could choose a huge demon. I was scared—shaking, bleeding, barely able to stand on my feet from the horrible things in the ceremony. I felt like I couldn't take much more, so I chose the demon. I had no idea what this choice meant yet, and I had no idea of what satan wanted from me. Much later I realised that this was exactly the choice satan wanted me to make. I found out that the demon would be with me for the rest of my life, and that it gave me powers. In the years

after this ceremony I kept gaining powers and learning to control them, and I believed satan's lies when he told me that he was my family and that I was special. I learned his lies very well, and I belonged to the top of satanism.

By the age of twenty, I lived in an apartment at college, and I wasn't doing well at all. I no longer wanted to live. God had oth-er plans for me and brought another college student across my path, Jimmy, who helped me discover what was really going on in my life. He helped me to get to know Jesus on a deep level and interact with Him. Together with Jesus, he helped me break out of satanism and endure my deliverance to the end. Now I am the lucky wife of this man, and I thank God for him every day.

After two extremely crazy and hard years of deliverance, break-ing free from satanism and constantly being attacked in the most absurd ways, the years of healing arrived to repair all the damage that was done. There were still attacks, but God taught us how to deal with them and gave us tools, as well. Every day, I expe-rienced more and more freedom on my healing journey. It was both a mental and physical battle. Lots of memories that I had locked away deep inside were coming back. When my body real-ized that I finally didn't have to fight so hard anymore, and that I was safe because the satanic rituals were finally over, I completely collapsed and couldn't sit up, not even to do a simple thing like go to the bathroom by myself. My husband stayed home with me and took care of me for four years. In the beginning, we prayed together every day. My husband prayed a lot for me, as well, as he does to this day on a regular basis. Jesus has been so very careful throughout this whole process. He always made sure that He didn't give me so much that I couldn't handle it anymore. It is like He has a very precise schedule where the correct order of doing things is written in the finest details. And if it felt like it was too much for me, I could feel Jesus very, very close to me, as He often navigated me through every detail. He always warned me when something very hard or big was about to come. And sometimes when I said, "Jesus! I can't handle it anymore!" I could feel two strong hands lifting me up, and before I knew it, I was sitting on God's lap, where peace would come over me that I cannot put into words.

I could never have dreamed of how I know Jesus now. I never knew that God is really so close and tangible, and that you can have such a wonderful relationship with Him. Jimmy and I knocked on many doors in search of help, but in the end, it became clear to me that Jesus was choosing to work through me and my husband. I go to Jesus every day and talk with Him face to face. He tells me exactly what to do, and He knows exactly what still needs to be done. The changes that I have undergone in recent years are huge! I am a totally different person, and God makes me completely new. I am slowly but surely becoming what He originally intended me to be.

This book may be about me, but all honor belongs to God. Jesus is never far away; He is always very close to you, even if you don't always experience it that way. Often I thought that it was too late and that it was better if my life ended. There is nothing so damaged that Jesus is unable to make it whole again—and it is never too late, either. Everything is possible for those who believe. I hope and pray that you will see and experience in your life that God is there for you the same as He was and is there for me.

This book started with a drawing. I had a strong feeling that I had to capture a moment I experienced with Jesus. Then Jesus made it clear to me that He wanted me to share the drawing on social media. I thought this was scary, but I did it anyway. It did not end with one drawing. I created more with Jesus, and God started challenging me to write the story behind every drawing. That was even scarier and seemed far too personal and vulnerable. I thought I couldn't really write, that I could not put my feelings, experiences, and thoughts into words at all. Jesus told me that I didn't have to worry about writing, and that He would do it together with me. What started with one drawing gradually became a series of drawings, and from a series of drawings came the command of God to make a book out of it—in Dutch and in English. I have written a lot of my healing process down in a diary. The stories are not fiction; they are real moments I captured. So this book is a bit like a journal with artwork.

I never thought I would ever write a book. I thought something like that would be the last thing I could do. And now it appears that I am not nearly finished yet, and that this is (only) my first book. I have drawings with little stories ready for the second book already. So you see . . . like I said: "Nothing is impossible for God. Just have faith and obey."

I will extol you, O Lord, for you have drawn me up and have not let my foes rejoice over
    me.
O Lord my God, I cried to you for help, and you have healed me.
O Lord, you have brought up my soul from Sheol; you restored me to life from among
    those who go down to the pit.
Sing praises to the Lord, O you his saints, and give thanks to his holy name.
For his anger is but for a moment, and his favor is for a lifetime. Weeping may tarry for the
    night, but joy comes with the morning.
As for me, I said in my prosperity, "I shall never be moved."
By your favor, O Lord, you made my mountain stand strong; you hid your face; I was dismayed.
To you, O Lord, I cry, and to the Lord I plead for mercy:
"What profit is there in my death, if I go down to the pit? Will the dust praise you? Will it tell of
    your faithfulness?
Hear, O Lord, and be merciful to me! O Lord, be my helper!"
You have turned for me my mourning into dancing; you have loosed my sackcloth and clothed
    me with gladness,
that my glory may sing your praise and not be silent. O Lord my God, I will give thanks to you
    forever!
—Psalm 30:1-12

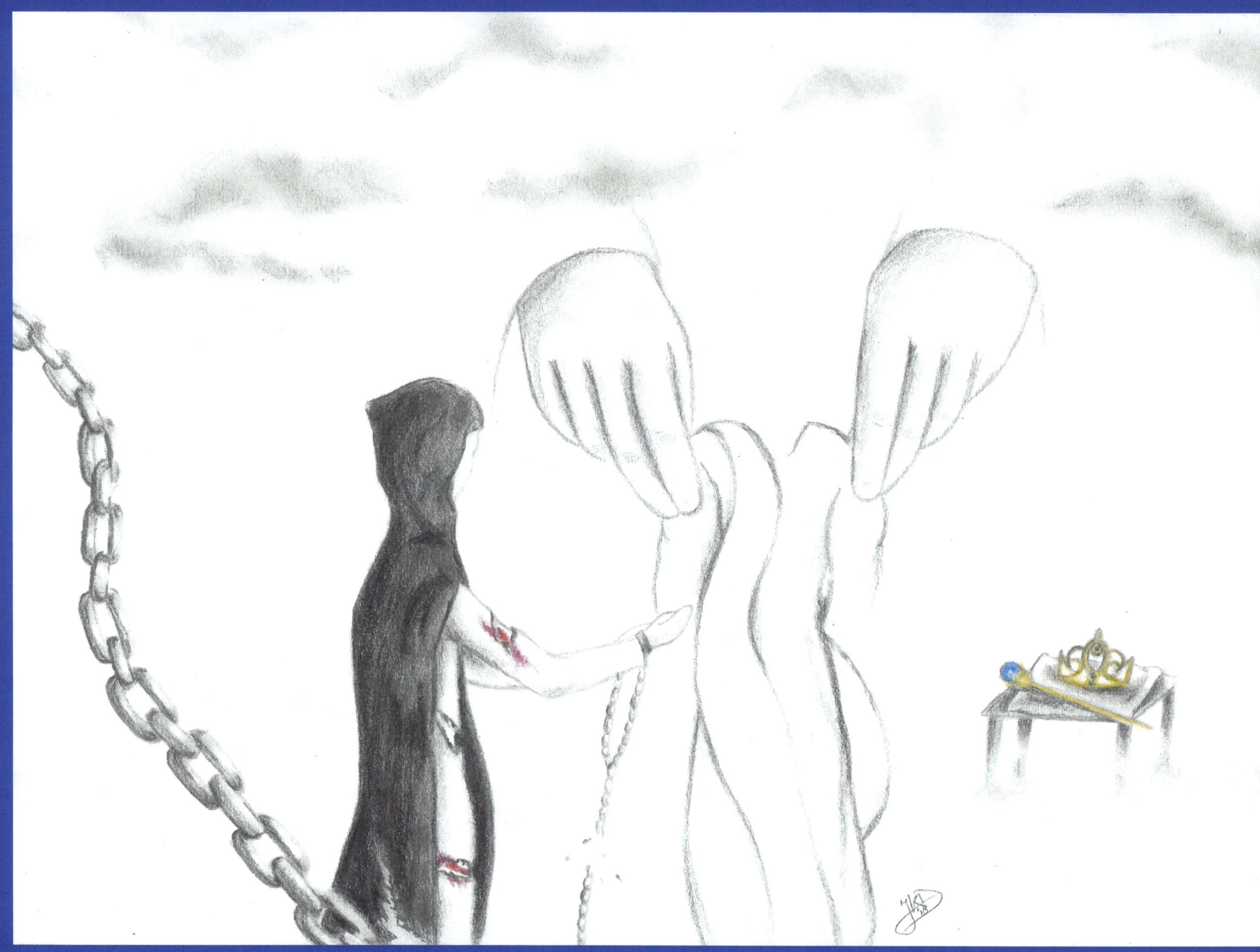

Jesus came, opened the doors, and rescued me
Demons could only watch me leave
I am free!

I thought I knew what freedom and power were, but it seems I really did not know much about that at all. I learned that Jesus doesn't need to force people to do anything in order to have power. Totally the opposite of what satan does! Jesus is greater and stronger than anything or anyone in this world. No matter what, He is King over this world, and He always will be. Satan makes people believe that he is god and that there is no one more powerful than he is. But one day, we will all see him and be surprised at how small he really is.

Jesus carries me to a place in heaven. There, He removes every chain from my body as if they are nothing. All this time, I believed being with satan was home, because that is what he always told me. But immediately I can feel that it is here, in this place, that I belong. It is hard to explain this, but instantly I know that I am home. I never felt anything like this before. I never knew I could feel something as wonderful and safe as this. I have returned to a place that I came from.

I look terrible. All the years of imprisonment, training, assault, mutation of my identity, and more—these have shaped me. I am left with terrible scars and wounds on me. I look as if I have been completely beaten. But Jesus is not shocked or worried at all. He shows me a white dress. Immediately I know that this dress represents a new identity . . . a new me. It is the person I was always meant to be.

Thank God it is never too late for Jesus to start over and completely renew a person. There is hope. I pray for all those people who don't know Jesus yet. You see, it doesn't matter where you are right now, what situation you are in, what you have done, nor what has been done to you. There is not one thing that can keep you from this loving person named Jesus. Nothing!

I know He is saying the same thing to you right now . . . "Please, come home."

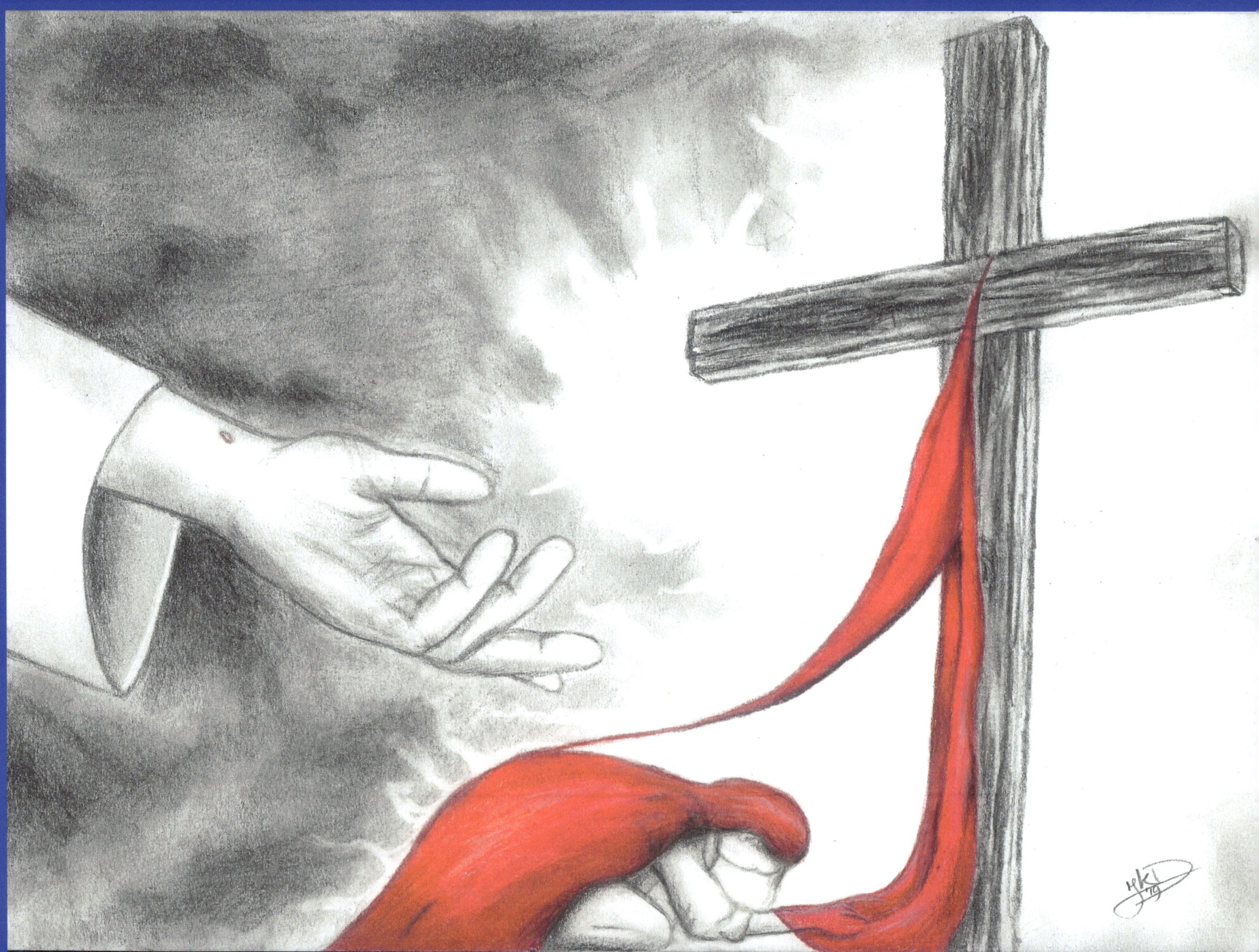

Covered

I don't want Jesus to come close to me. Every time He does, I drop down on my knees and stare at the floor. One day, when I am trying to pull away from His nearness, He helps me get up as He looks lovingly into my eyes and says, "Dear child, you must stop doing this." But I do not understand what He wants from me. I feel so bad about myself. I cannot seem to grasp His love, and I feel so strongly that I do not deserve Him. Oh yes—I am thankful He rescued me, but I keep imagining myself somewhere in the back of the line, where I feel I belong. Far away from Jesus.

He is constantly coming so close to me, and I have a hard time understanding why He is doing this . . . why He—this big, mighty, and holy God—wants to be around me. Jesus asks me, "Are you not happy with what I did for you?" Well, yes, I am happy. He continues, "Yes, I died for the world, but you must realize this: I died for *you*. And that was because I wanted to. Will you accept that?" I can see that He is sincere. I decide to accept His sacrifice for me and believe that He wants to come close to me and be with me, although I still don't quite understand it all.

This decision is changing my life. I am starting to grow closer to Jesus and have a real relationship with Him. It is because of what He did on the cross that He could rescue me. Because of His blood I have hope, and I can have a beautiful future where I am completely free and healed. He doesn't even look at my past. He has already paid for all the mistakes, the things I wish had never happened. I guess seeing what I will become is a lot more important to Him than looking at my past. His plans for my life are amazing. He is trying to show me that He loves me very much— and not only that, but I am royalty.

As I continue to grow closer to Him, I reflect on some things. He proved that I was worth dying for. He went to hell for me. I may never completely understand His willingness to suffer and die for me, but I have been given a treasured gift. I now know and understand there is no safer feeling than to be so close to Him. Nothing exceeds the assurance that I now have, that I am completely loved and safe. The most powerful thing on earth covers me, and it is His precious blood.

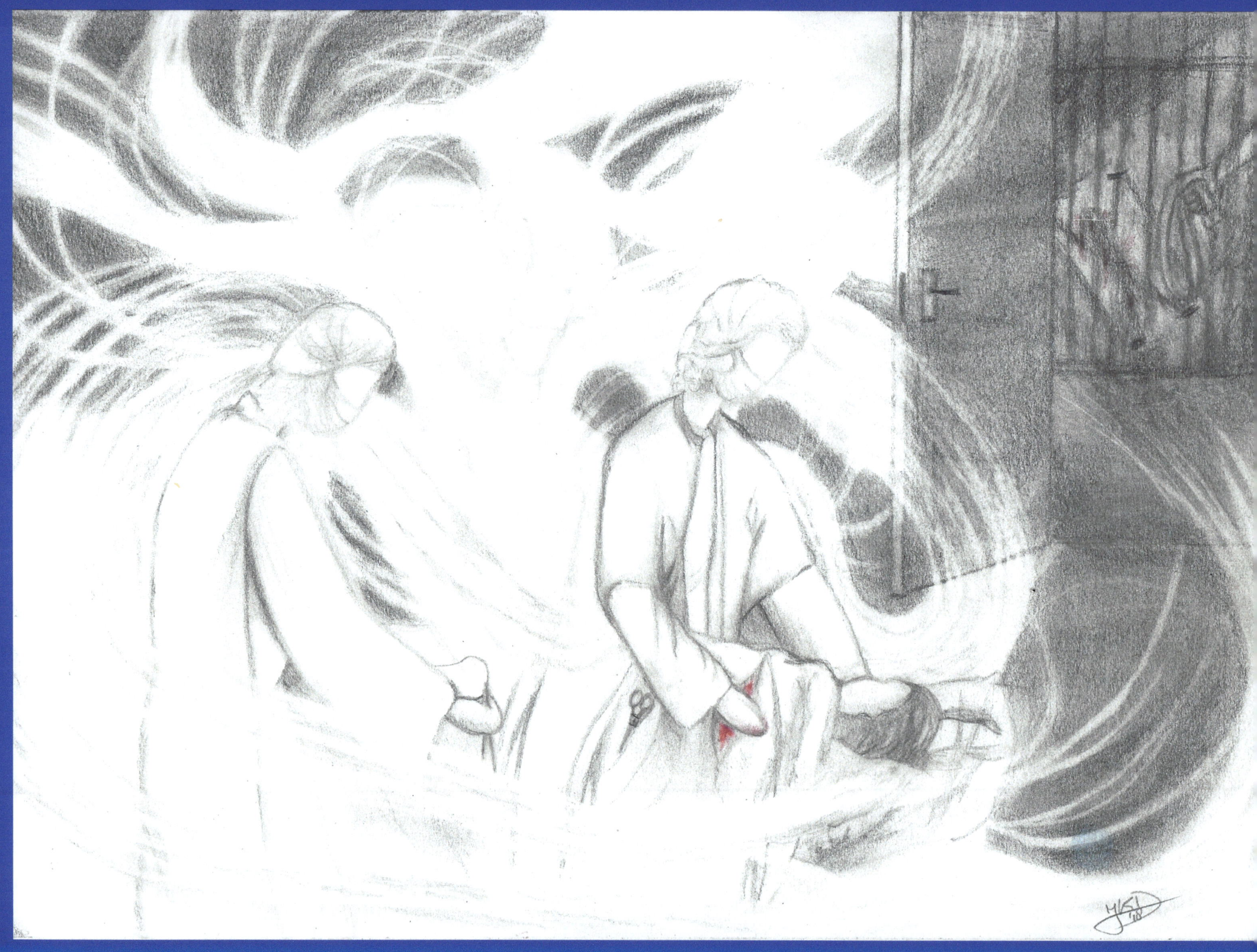

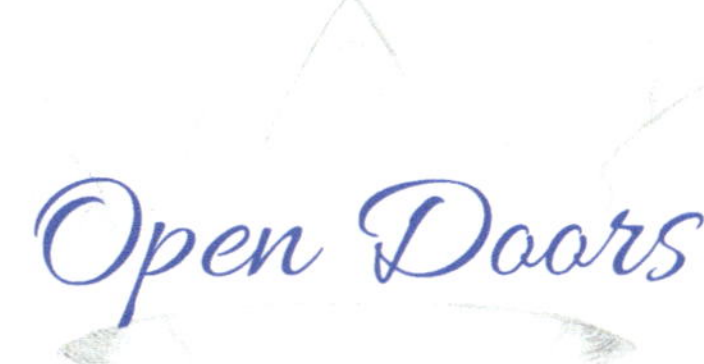

Open Doors

There is this very long hallway with lots and lots of doors in it. Jesus asks me if I am ready. And I answer Him: "Let's get this over with." He knows what is behind every door; I don't know anymore. They call it repressed memories.

We walk to one of the doors and open it. When we go into the dark space that was locked behind it, I know I will be going back to the past—but this time, I am safe with Jesus. I am holding His hand, and all of a sudden everything that has been locked up is coming back to me, crashing over me like a wave . . .

After awhile, Jesus tells me it is enough for now, and He carries me to a table. I see God and I see the Holy Spirit. I am ready for them to perform surgery again. I guess they will cut open an old wound and clean it so it will heal properly. It's extremely painful. I can feel everything again—emotionally and physically. It is really hard, and it will continue to be like this for awhile, but I know that the most gentle hands are leading and healing me so I will be able to close the door again. This time forever.

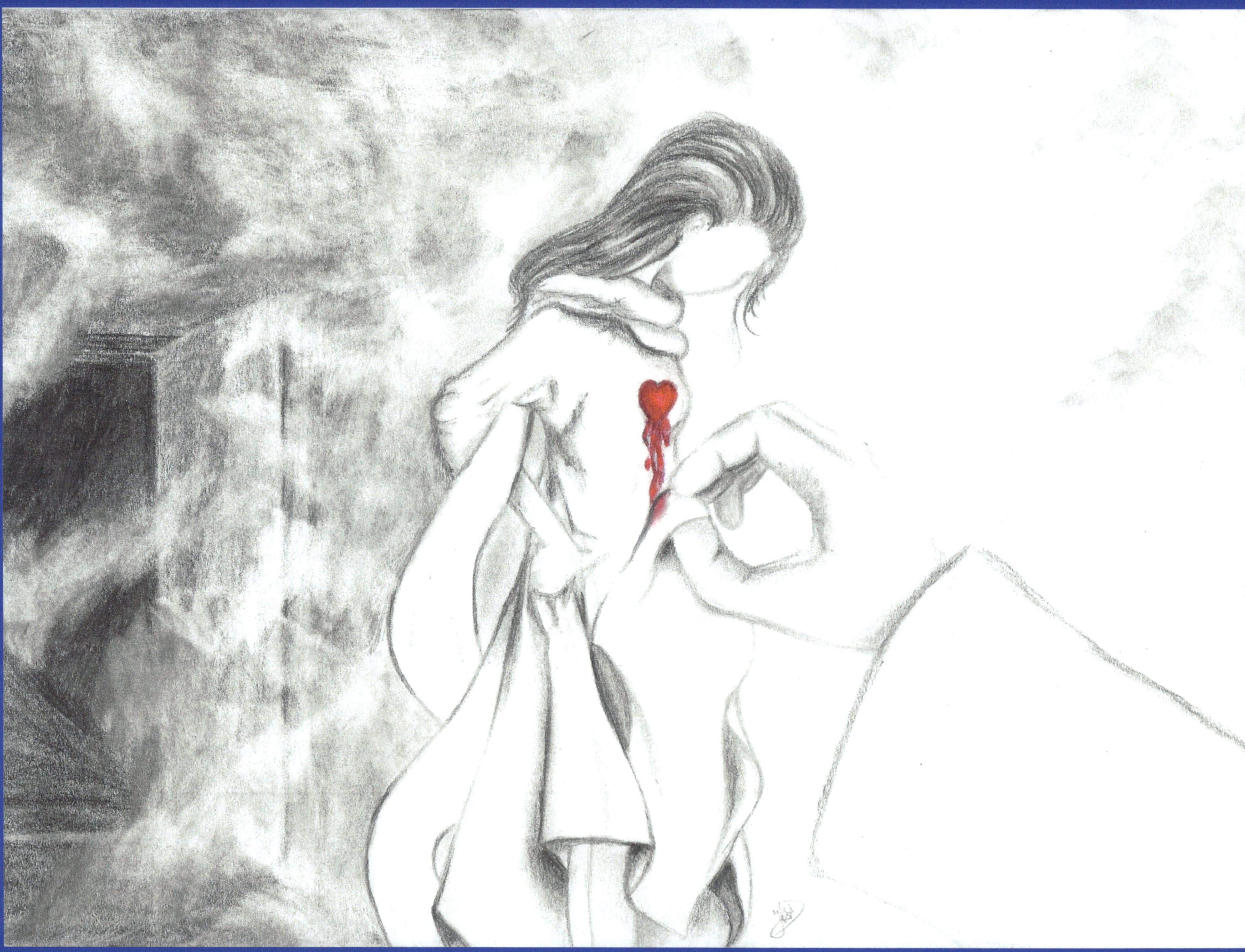

Jesus, Healer

It hurts. I don't want to get up and start the day. The night terrors I have when I sleep don't help, either. I feel worthless, and I don't see the meaning of living right now. I think about going to Jesus. Nothing helps me feel better in periods like this—except Jesus. Only Jesus can help. I focus on Him, and I don't have to wait long to see Him. I talk with Jesus lots of times. I can do that with Him whenever I want to. I just have to go to Him.

Jesus is there waiting for me, and I can see Him wringing out a soft white cloth in a bowl filled with water. He walks towards me with the wet cloth, and as I look down, I see blood running down my chest. Jesus does not say a word. Gently, He starts cleaning me. Tears are streaming down my face.

It is ok to feel this way.

A couple of minutes later, I am in my bedroom again—and I feel better. Not great, but better. Ready to start the day.

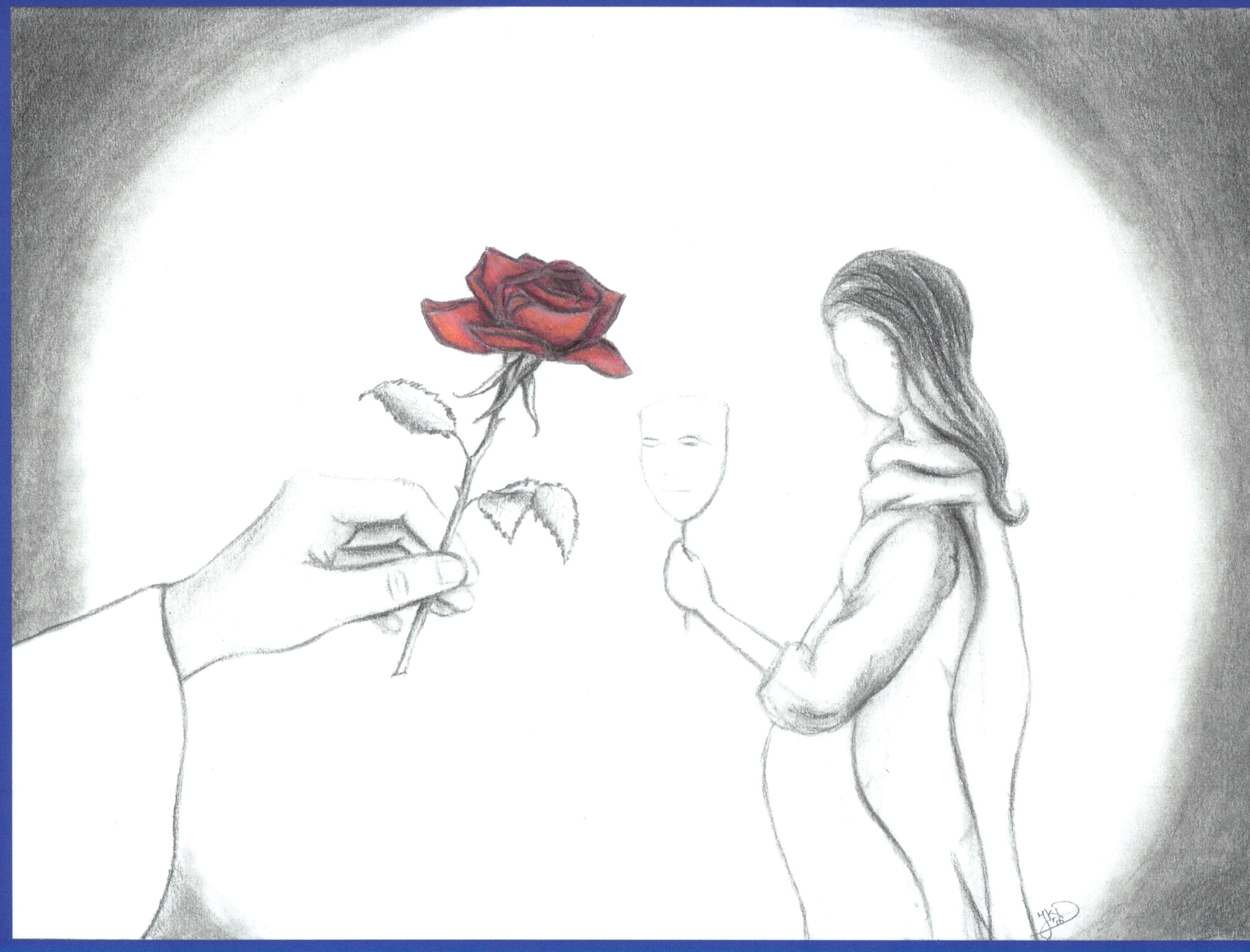

The Romance

It is weird . . .

I did not even know who I was before, so I was playing a role my whole life based on who I thought I was. But now that I live so closely with Jesus, I am starting to see who I really am, and that the things I made my own (like acting strong all the time and thinking I didn't need anyone's help) is not good, not healthy, not the way Jesus wants it to go. He knows who I really am anyway. And I am starting to see that I don't need to act that role out anymore, although it is still hard to let it go. I don't know how to act without it. It is scary, and I feel vulnerable. I always thought I was strong, but now I am starting to see and learn that I am not. Not at all. And even stranger . . . I do not even need to be strong myself. Jesus is strong in me when I am weak, and that's much better and healthier. It sounds illogical, but it is a big and strong weapon. I am the strongest when He is strong in me during these moments. That's totally different than just believing yourself, that you are strong!

Getting to know Jesus more and more is like discovering a world of opposites—the opposite of what I always learned and the opposite about myself. It will take a while for me to completely get it all, but it suits a lot better to who I am. And it makes me much more beautiful than I could ever have imagined.

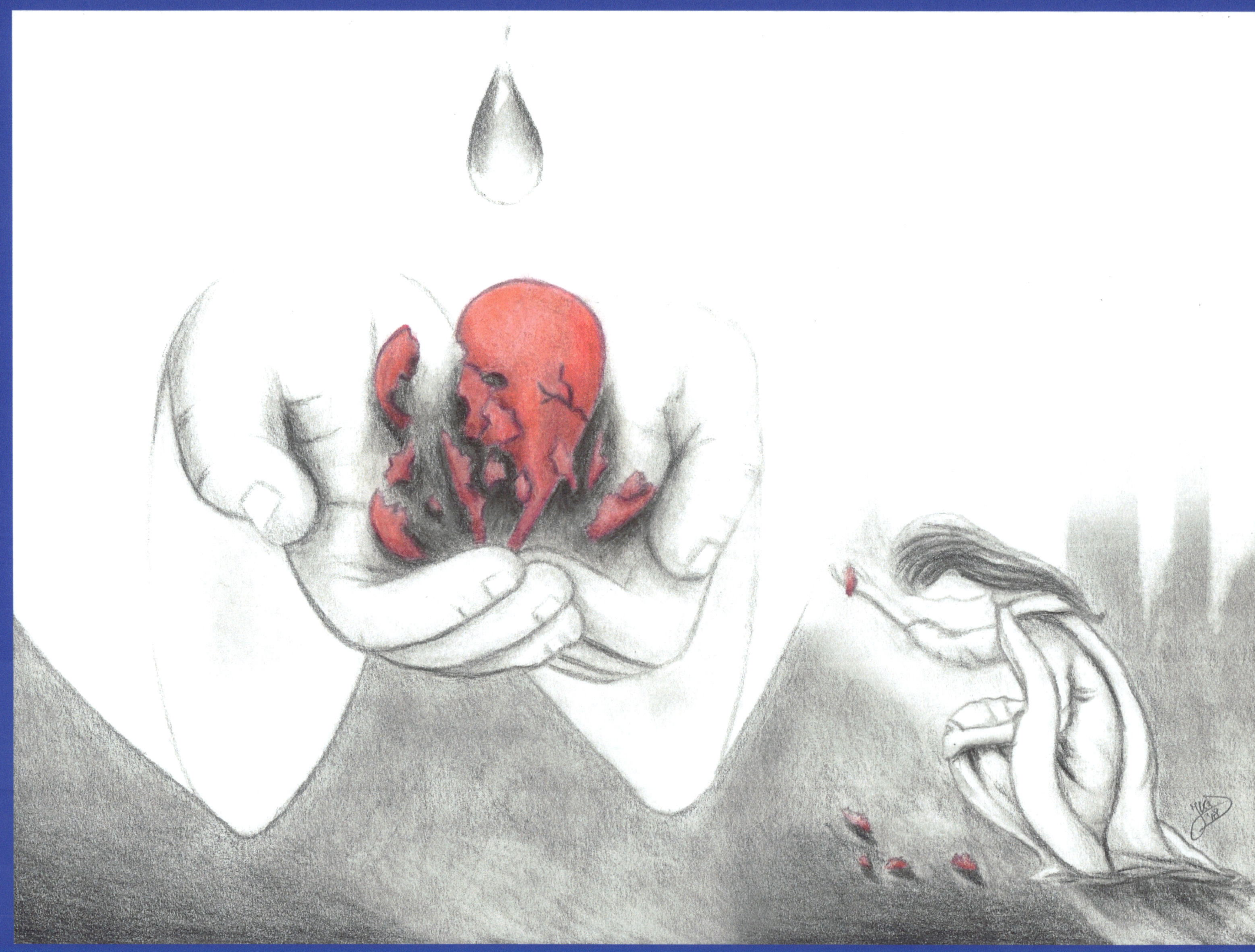

I feel all alone. There is nobody here. I don't know what to do anymore, and I feel sad. I feel like Jesus is very far away from me. I try to talk with Him, but it doesn't really seem to work. I don't hear His voice. I feel like I am always alone when I feel the worst about myself. Of course, that's not true, so I try to remember that—but I give up trying to hear His voice and just sit on the couch, staring in front of me.

After awhile, I start seeing a floor that is so smooth and clean, it almost looks like a mirror. In the distance, I think I see something on the floor. I decide to walk toward it, and after a while I discover that it is Jesus. I have never seen Him like this before. He is sitting on the floor, and when I come a bit closer I see little pieces lying on the floor in front of Him. They are little pieces of my heart! I'm surprised, yet somehow I recognized the pieces straightaway. Jesus is gently picking them up, one by one. It looks like a piece of glass fell on the floor and has shattered into a lot of pieces.

When I shift my attention to Jesus, I can see that He is crying. Tears are streaming down His face as He gently gathers all the pieces. I can hear the tears dripping on the floor, one by one . . . Suddenly I can feel very deeply that if my heart breaks, Jesus' heart breaks, too. Right now He is feeling what I am feeling—maybe even more deeply than I feel it. I kneel down to help Him. I personally want to hand Him the pieces and say, "Jesus, I trust you. Here is my heart. I know You are the only One who can and will make it whole again. Thank You for always being there for me."

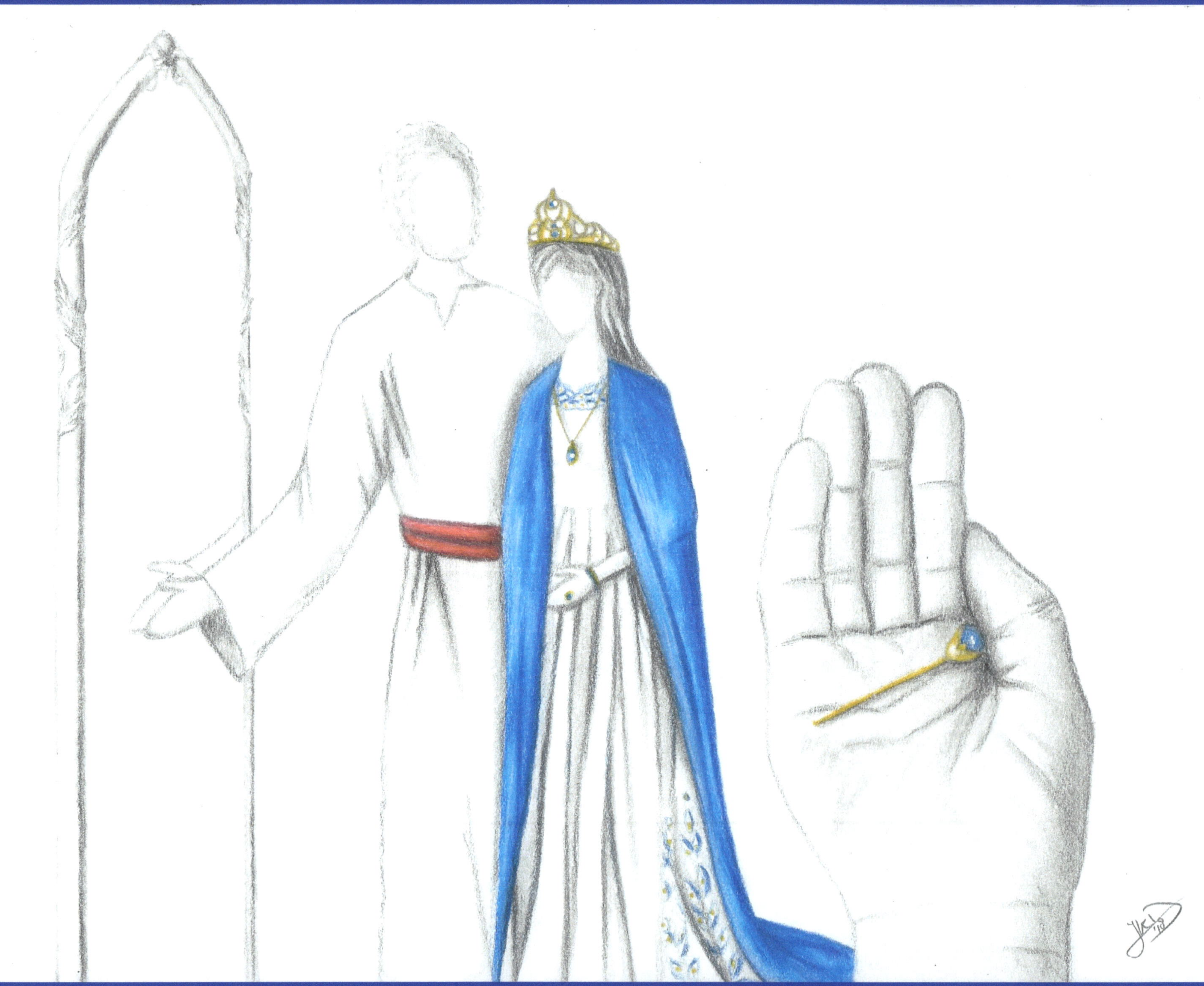

Just Me

I feel empty. I gave everything I had to Jesus. Nothing is what it seemed to be. I have been living a lie my whole life. Who am I? Everything I thought I was, wasn't me. They took my heart, broke it, and replaced the pieces. Another identity, another me. They were only lies. *Who am I?* Why am I even here? I know I did the right thing by giving everything to Jesus, but I feel like there is nothing left of me now.

There is Jesus, and He is smiling at me. "I know who you are," He says. "I knew all along, since the day I made you. Come with Me and I'll show you."

There is a huge mirror, and I am standing right in front of it. First I look to Jesus, He seems to be very proud and happy. Then I look in the mirror, and all I see is beauty and royalty. I feel confused. He takes my hand and says, "Don't worry—the day will come when you don't need a mirror and you will see it yourself. Just trust Me."

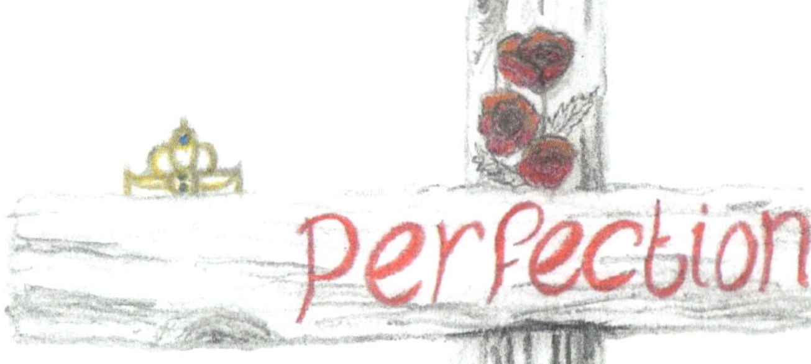

Perfection
Defeat
Worthless
Hopelessness
Rejection

The Choice

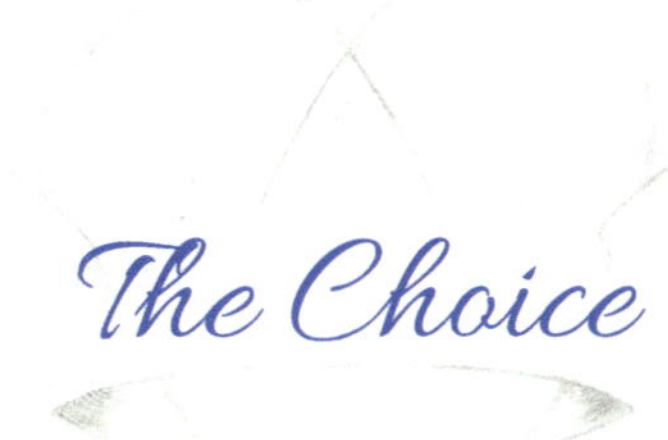

"Satan, I am so tired of you interfering with my life. I don't care what you make up about me this time. You want to hold me back from being the way I really am. I know what does and doesn't belong to me, even if the things you whisper feel like they do belong to me."

I don't want his lies, his messing with my feelings and my hurt anymore. So it is simple: from now on, only positive thoughts belong to me. I have a choice, and I know this choice doesn't have to match with what I feel inside. I can be strong and know that I am never a victim because I cannot be a victim and a conqueror in Christ at the same time.

I know Your promises, Jesus, are true, and that You make all things new. Whether I see it or not, You do. And these promises You gave me, I hold so tightly that I will never lose them or let anyone take them from me. With Jesus, I always win. "So I choose each day, satan, and I just dance your lies away."

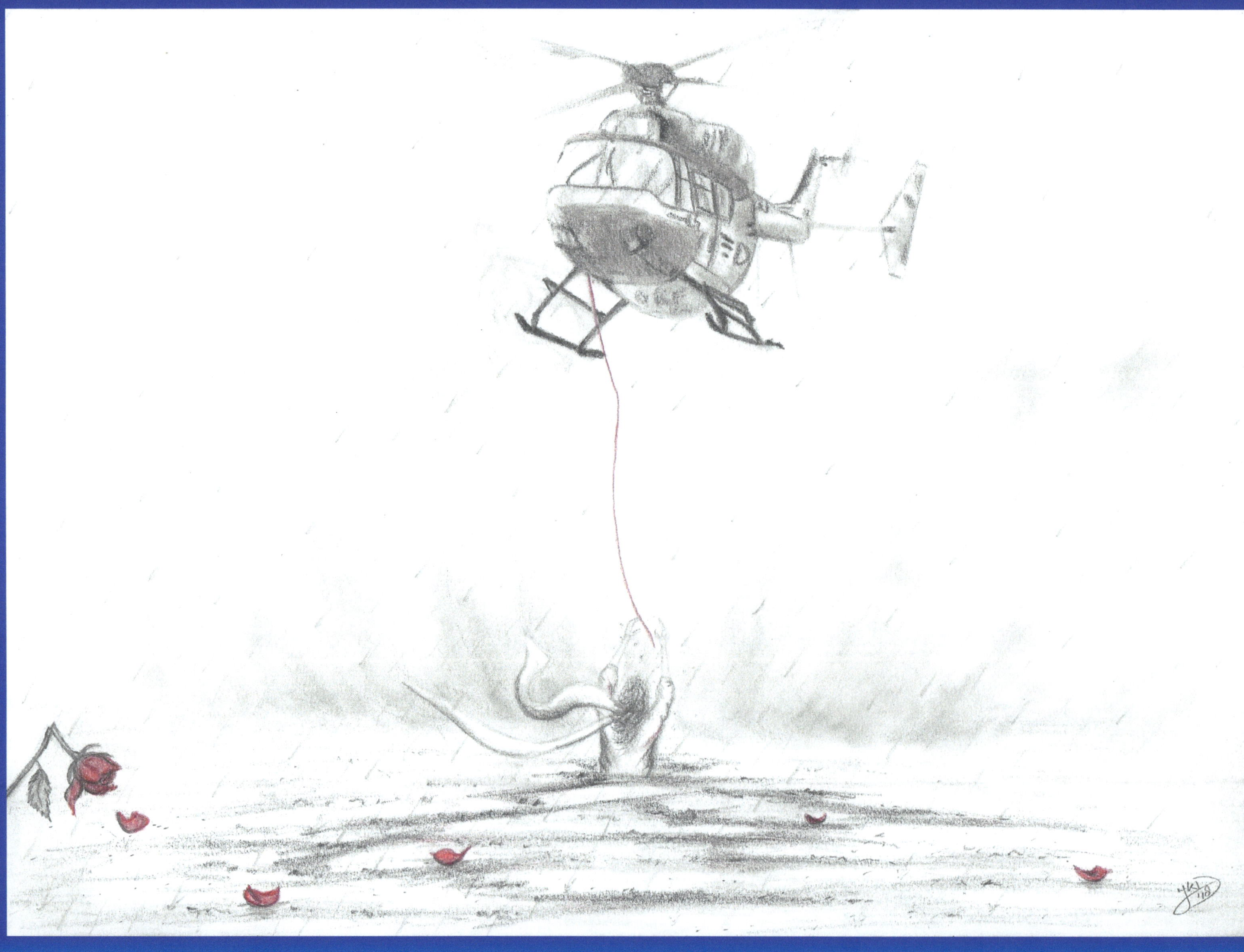

Filthy Ocean

I can't see where it ends, and I can't see where it starts. The only thing I see is this filthy ocean I'm in. I want to get out but I don't know how. Every time I move to try to get out of it, I'm sinking deeper, and it hurts so much I want to die. How can I ever live again? I'm stuck . . . There is so much hate inside of me. If it was up to me, I would kill all men on this planet. I've been molested all my life until now, but it feels like it never stopped because I am reliving it again every day. Why do they call God a father, and why is Jesus a man? Don't you understand I can never trust man again?

I can cry, I can scream, I can be angry—but I will always be alone. The only thing I will hear is this empty echo coming back at me.

I can't take this anymore, so, Jesus, if you really love me and I can trust You, I want to try. Everything inside of me screams "No!"—but I choose to at least try to trust You.

"You cannot do this alone," Jesus says when I see Him. He is flying above the ocean, looking at the ugly mess I'm in. He throws out a red rope and I grab it. Before I realize what just happened, I am with Jesus. The pain is still there . . . but the hate is not. I am not in the ocean anymore. I didn't do that, He did. It is such a relief. I guess a man who loves me so much that He died for me has a lot of patience, and He understands more than I can myself. He can do anything.

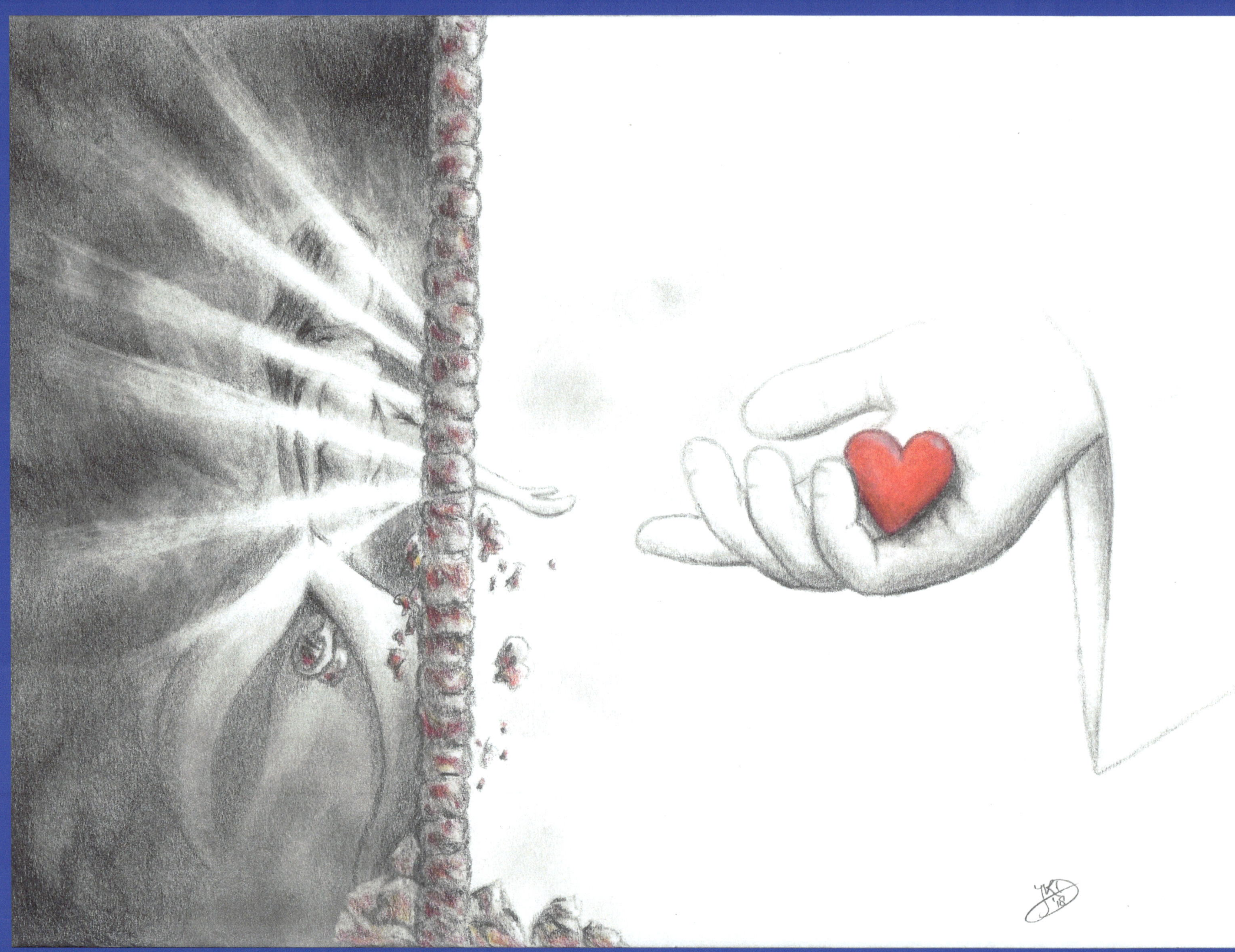

The Power of Love

My childhood wasn't easy. When I was about six or seven years old, I had already gone through so many traumas that one day I decided to never be afraid anymore. I wanted to feel nothing—or at least never show anyone my feelings. The moment I decided this, my heart turned into a cold stone. When people tormented me or did other things, I just looked right into their eyes and laughed in their faces. I believed the lie I created that nobody could ever hurt me again.

When I broke out of satanism, I met my husband. He took me in and protected me 24/7. Everyone except his roommates told him to stop protecting me, but he wouldn't. People told him it was too dangerous, it was an attack from satan, he wouldn't finish his studies. It exhausted him. But he simply believed that freedom in Christ was for everyone—including me. He prayed for me day and night. He stayed awake while I slept. It confused me; I had never seen eyes filled with so much compassion. They were eyes filled with the love of Jesus. Nobody could ever reach me, but I literally saw his eyes shining like lights through all the darkness that was surrounding me like a cloud. I never wanted anybody to take care of me, but I had no choice, since I was very ill. Most of the time I could not walk, and sometimes I couldn't even say one word.

As time went by, it became clear to both of us that God didn't just put us together for this process—we were meant to stay together our whole lives. After about six months together, I was home alone . . . and my husband came back just in time. He helped me out of the puddle of blood I was in and put me in bed. While he sat next to me on the edge of the bed, he looked at me and I saw a lot of emotion in his eyes. After a few minutes, he broke the silence and said, "I love you." From the second he told me that, there was a fierce battle going on inside of me. After a while (it felt like forever), I managed to say, "I love you, too . . ." I had *never* said this to anyone in my life. The moment I spoke these words, a huge wall around my heart came crashing down. If you knew my whole story, you probably wouldn't expect me to say that this was the biggest breakthrough I ever experienced—but it absolutely was. I felt Jesus' arms hugging me, and they just didn't let go.

That week I cried and cried and cried . . . I couldn't stop. Something in my heart came alive that day.

If I speak in the tongues of men and of angels, but have
    not love, I am a noisy gong or a clanging cymbal.
    And if I have prophetic powers, and understand all
    mysteries and all knowledge, and if I have all faith, so as
    to remove mountains, but have not love, I am nothing.
If I give away all I have, and if I deliver up my body to be
    burned, but have not love, I gain nothing.
Love is patient and kind; love does not envy or boast; it is not
    arrogant or rude.
It does not insist on its own way; it is not irritable or resent-
    ful; it does not rejoice at wrongdoing, but rejoices with
    the truth.

Love bears all things,

    believes all things,

        hopes all things,

            endures all things.

Love never ends.

As for prophecies, they will pass away; as for tongues, they
    will cease; as for knowledge, it will pass away.
For we know in part and we prophesy in part, but when the
    perfect comes, the partial will pass away.
When I was a child, I spoke like a child, I thought like a
    child, I reasoned like a child. When I became a man, I
    gave up childish ways.
For now we see in a mirror dimly, but then face to face.
Now I know in part; then I shall know fully, even as I have
    been fully known.
So now faith, hope, and love abide, these three; but the great-
    est of these is love.

–1 Corinthians 13 (ESV)

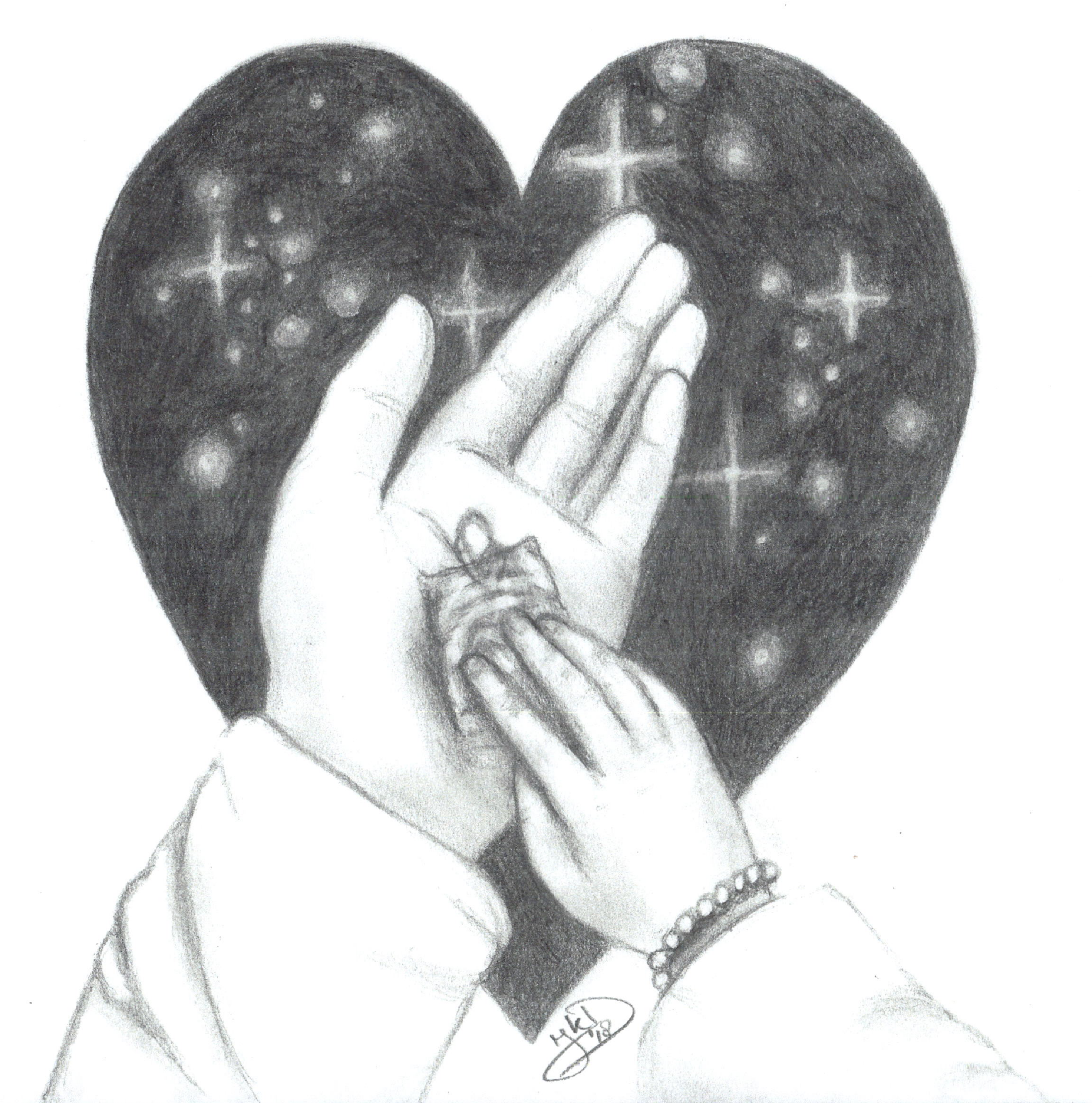

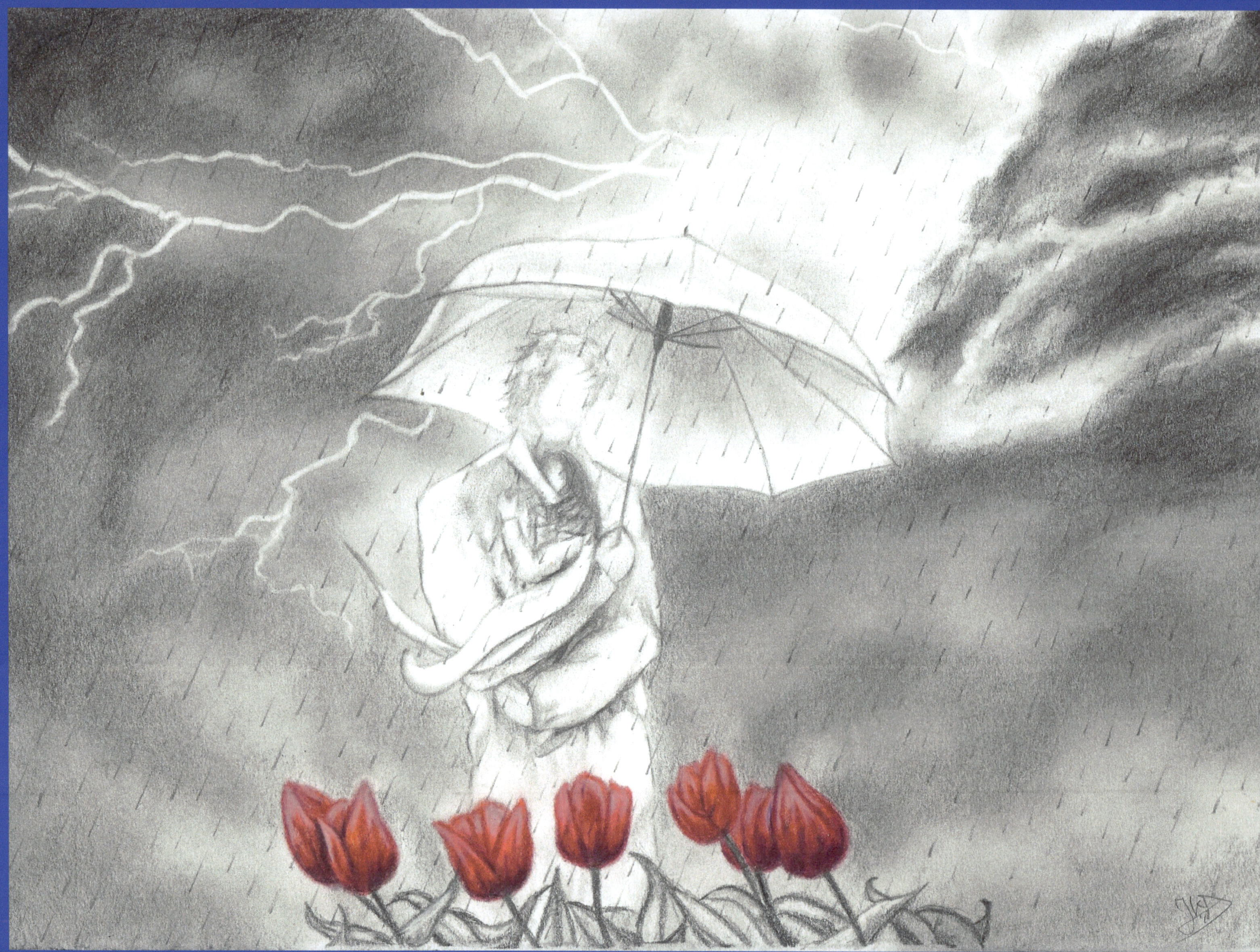

Back in Time with Jesus

I am playing in a field with lots of flowers. I love flowers—I can look at them all day. They have lost a bit of color because of drought, but that doesn't bother me. I am a little child, and Jesus is watching me like a parent.

After awhile, He calls my name and points with His finger towards the sky. Big dark clouds are coming closer and closer, and I hear thunder in the distance. I assume Jesus will take me inside . . . but He doesn't. He has an umbrella with Him, and He takes me in His strong arms. "We are not going inside. You are strong and brave enough to go through this storm with Me," He says. I hide in His thick, warm coat while the rain is pouring down. The wind is blowing hard and lightning is everywhere. The flowers are coming more and more back to life, but I don't see it. I don't see anything, I feel like all I can do is hold on tight to Jesus. Moments are going through my head where I felt alone, betrayed, and abandoned by everyone, including Jesus. I feel sad and angry and afraid.

But after a while I realize . . . While I am going through all these memories again, He is closer now than He ever was before. Jesus tells me when the storm is over I will feel safer and less afraid. And I know I will be held by Him, whatever will come my way. Things will never be like they were before.

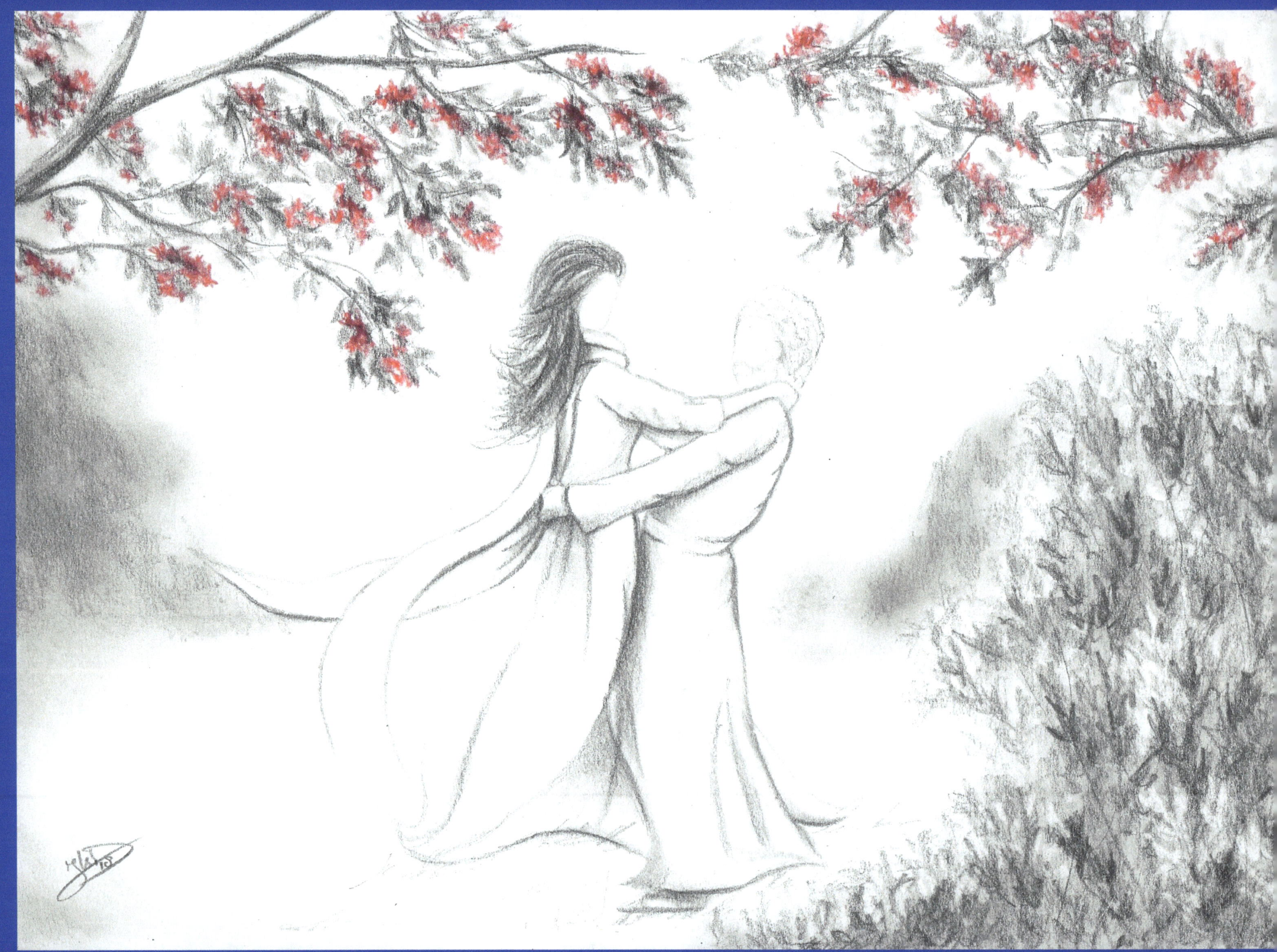

Fun with Jesus

S ometimes it feels very overwhelming. All the things I need to work on, everything I struggle with. So much I still need to change about myself . . .

While I am sitting and thinking about these things, I feel someone touching me. I lift up my head and look right into Jesus' eyes. He is smiling at me and holding out His hand to help me stand up and go with Him. I accept His invitation, and we start walking. After awhile, He stops, turns Himself to me, and starts dancing with me. At first, it feels a little uncomfortable, but soon it is going very smoothly and I only have to look at Him. I don't think about anything anymore; all I see is Jesus. I feel joy coming up from inside of me. If there is one thing I have learned, it is to surrender everything to Jesus and trust that He knows what needs to be done. No trying hard myself all the time. That's just exhausting.

This was a big key for me when I learned this. I tell Jesus what I struggle with, give it to Him, give myself to Him, and give Him permission to change things in me. Then I let it go.

He will make the change. We only need to look at Jesus and wait.

I am filled with thankfulness to everyone who has prayed for me, to everyone who has touched my life, and to everyone I have learned from. Whether we are connected in person or you are supporting me on social media, thank you.

I want to take some time to thank Lin Jane Maynard who has helped me with everything I wrote to make sure the English version is good, as well as all her suggestions and patience during this process. I am thankful for her always being so loving and kind. Her encouraging words with the making of this book, as well as her comments that were written under the artwork I posted on social media, have built me up.

Especially a big thank you to my husband for all his patience with me, his prayers with and for me, and his amazing love for me, God, and others. He was the one sent by God to guide me out of satanism, and he taught me so much about God. Everyone told him to stop praying for me and to stop taking care of me, but he didn't listen. Through all the protests of everyone around us, he kept being faithful to God and me. When we searched for help and every door closed in our faces, he stayed with me and never stopped praying, never gave up. There were times we experienced God's greatness, love, and power, and there were times we wondered where God was and if He had forgotten about us. We cried together with tears of immense pain and tears of pure joy. We discovered that God had put us together for more than this adventure—we will share our lives together until we die. So this way I want to show my enormous gratitude to Jimmy—my husband, my closest friend, and my hero.

And of course thanks and praise be to Jesus for not giving up on me, for setting me free, and for continuing to heal me until I am completely renewed. His love and faithfulness last for a lifetime. He is the only One who can turn bad into good, ashes into beauty, mourning into dancing. Through this journey, I received something that I never dared to dream. I never knew someone could have such a close and intimate relationship with God, where He guides your every step, shows you exactly what needs to be done in the healing journey, and heals completely. I talk with Jesus every day. Some times have been hard, and I have had days and nights where I couldn't think of anything else than dying and being apart from myself because what I felt inside was unbearable. But God never let go of my hand. He always knew exactly what He was doing and, as a result, I am a completely different person! Through this crazy journey, I received something priceless, something I never would have had. Jesus absolutely knows how to turn everything into good and to make it beautiful. I don't have enough words to express how thankful I am.

Judith Kayadoe was born in Groningen, the Netherlands. She is the founder of Royalty Fine Art, a christian-based art business/ministry, which is rooted from when Judith discovered how to create prophetic art with Jesus. God used art to aid her healing process, and now He is also using her to bring healing to others through her art. Jesus is Judith's physician who personally heals her from all the deep traumas that have arisen during the years she was trapped in satanism.

God has spoken to Judith several times about writing books in the past, and Judith never really knew what to do with this. But despite having no desire to write, God already had in mind that she would write books, so slowly this book journey has become reality.

Website: www.royaltyfineart.com
Email: judith@royaltyfineart.com
Facebook: Judith Kayadoe Royalty Fine Art
Instagram: @judith_royaltyfineart

Thank you for reading my book! I hope you enjoyed it and that it spoke to you.

I am a full-time artist, and I love to make prophetic art. But the drawings in this book are different. Mostly I paint or draw for other people, but these drawings came from a very personal and intimate time with Jesus where He was working on my healing. This artwork has a very unique purpose. If a specific drawing speaks to you, you can purchase it as a print or a card. Not only did these drawings bring healing to me, I created them together with Jesus for other people, as well. I think that is why Jesus wanted me to share these on social media, where I have received a lot of beautiful messages from people around the world.

If God has brought you encouragement or healing or has done something in you through this book, I would love to hear your testimony, if you would like to share it with me. You may send an email or visit my social media channels to see more artwork and connect with me.